THE LIBRARY
OF
THE UNIVERSITY
OF CALIFORNIA
LOS ANGELES

The
Revolution in Germany

A Study including separate Essays entitled
That Dictatorship of the Proletariat
and Revolutionary Socialism and the
Constituent Assembly in Germany

By
KARL DANNENBERG

Reprint from the January-March, 1919, issue of
The Radical Review

The Radical Review Publishing Association
202 East Seventeenth Street, New York City

Price Ten Cents

The Revolution in Germany

When the last of crowns like glass shall break
On the scene our sorrows have haunted,
And the People the last dread "guilty" shall speak,
On your side ye shall find me undaunted,
On Rhine, or on Danube, in word and deed,
Ye shall witness, true to his vow,
On the wrecks of thrones, in the midst of the freed,
The rebel who greets you now!

(From the "Farewell of the 'Neue Rheinische Zeitung',"
May 19th, 1849, by Ferdinand Freiligrath.)

I.

UPON this writing the Republic or at least a constitutional form of government seems assured in Germany. As the various social layers become more thoroughly permeated with the principles and immediate effects of this to the average German so gigantic and momentous upheaval, the possibilities of a successful counter-revolution become evermore remote. Also as the shadow of the Allies' armies, the democratic minions, on the border or within the fatherland becomes more distinct and grows bolder, the harassing menace of a monarchic coup d'état slowly diminishes and gradually disappears. Without exaggeration, it seems that the feudal barnacles, which have for centuries so tenaciously clung to the German body politic, and which finally served so ably as submissive, pliable agents of an aggressive Imperialism, aiming to establish an international oligarchy, have at last been amputated by the recently inaugurated revolution culminating out of the economic ruins produced by nigh five years of wanton destruction and unproductive consumption. Therefore, the so belated political Renaissance now embracing the native land of Goethe, Kant, Wagner and Marx, a Renaissance whose first manifestations in 1848-49 were so brutally stifled with the aid of the Russian soldiery, can at least be considered one of the few substantial products whose completion was tremendously hastened and whipped on by this unparalleled holocaust.

When, however, studying in this connection the general agencies of publicity and particularly the Socialist press, we find that no unity of opinion prevails, especially in the appraisal of the historic significance, possibilities and tangible immediate achievements of the Revolution. The popular view in the Socialist camp, a view expressed with a great and mainly sentimental enthusiasm at innumerable monster demonstrations, is to conceive and classify the German Revolution as a proletarian rebellion, a *social* revolution, and to define the present Government either as Socialist, or as the appropriate instrument of the Socialist Republic strenuously clamoring for birth. And as many of these definitions and opinions have subsequently appeared in representative Socialist journals, with recognized "leaders" for their authors, we are compelled to admit that they can be treated as everything else but the rantings or vaporings of irresponsible individuals. Therefore, we can state, without exaggeration, that to many Socialists the proclamation and organization of the Republic in Germany has been synonymous with the inauguration of the Industrial Republic; to others, the successful establishment of a constitutional government, or at least the radical removal of the feudal obstacles to such a government, of course, always taking the peculiar and to them exceedingly favorable social condition as a basis for their opinion, seems only the preparatory act to an early consummation of the Socialist Commonwealth; again others entertain the somewhat unpopular view that the recent Revolution is not so much the product of a premeditated, organized, class-conscious activity of the working class, as it is an act of absolute economic necessity and self-preservation on the part of class-conscious German Imperialism; and that, therefore, it is primarily a bourgeois revolution, animated by and following *immediate* bourgeois interests, and only, secondarily, a proletarian uprising governed by and running a proletarian course. Advancing the last conception as our own, we presume it is needless to emphasize that we consider the first two views to be defective and out of joint with the actual facts of current historic events. However, in line with scientific investigation and discussion, the duty now falls upon us to establish a sound and defensible foundation for our contention; if successful, formulating the necessary historic, sociological and economic premises and principles substantiating the first affirmed deduction, and thereby disproving the first two versions.

If the recent Revolution in Germany has, therefore, either established a Socialist Republic, or the basis for such a republic, and will shortly culminate into a Socialist Commonwealth, then it is certainly logical and imperative to conclude: That the Revolution which overthrew the existing government was primarily or essentially a class-conscious proletarian revolution dominated by a Socialist objective. Does the deduction, flowing from the

2

above two propositions, square with historic facts? Was the dominant power wielded by the Revolution chiefly generated by Socialist or working-class aspirations and aims; did the propelling forces, the inherent basic vitality underlying this momentous social cataclysm, draw their strength from an appeal to the class interests of the proletariat? Or was the immediate objective of the Revolution, i. e., the overthrow of monarchy, actuated and dictated in the first place by the unrelenting forces of economic necessity and self-preservation, and, therefore, formulated, striven for and realized, not because it was born of a great national desire, aiming to fulfil a glorious ideal left unrealized in 1848, but because the social conditions in Germany had taken on certain threatening forms a few months prior to the outbreak; forms and characteristics which contained not only a significant lesson for German Imperialism, but which also had a more than ominous warning for its very existence as a ruling class bound up with it? Let me proceed to calmly examine the historic material and data at our disposal, in order to be able to arrive at intelligent conclusions so imperative for a proper answer to the above questions.

The sudden and really unexpected and insistent solicitation of peace terms by the Central powers was, we believe, at first even a surprise to the best informed strategists and diplomats of the Allies. The subsequent and unconditional acceptance of the stringent terms imposed by the Allies upon Germany for an armistice was a still greater source of bewilderment to many. And when, to cap the climax, the Revolution within followed this great military debacle, sweeping feudal prerogatives and monarchical pomp, together with all other medieval barnacles and seemingly antiquated social superstructures, into oblivion, many a student of contemporary history held his head—momentarily dazed by the force of this avalanche of problems.

What forces brought the German military machine, this veritable Octopus, which had never suffered a decisive defeat, after resting upon the laurels of a relatively successful offensive, and occupying strategically choice positions a stone's throw away from the heart of France, to the brink of such a humiliating surrender? What powerful factors compelled the German Imperialists to negotiate and accept an armistice that actually placed their military power and basic economic resources into the hands of their most bitter foes? For instance, what compelling circumstances led to the surrender of the cream of the German navy—without a shot; or to the surrender of Germany's most efficient artillery, largest percentage of rolling stock and other instruments of industry and warfare? What important and inexorable necessity could have compelled these class-conscious Imperialists to widely open their boundaries to their arch competitors, by evacuating for Allied occupation the most important and strongest

3

Gibraltars in Germany? Was it the fear for a revolution from within that prompted these members of the capitalist class to solicit a compact with their erstwhile competitors against the rising proletariat? Did the German Imperialists know that the jig was up, and, therefore, to save what could be saved of moribund Capitalism, attempt to capitulate rather to the Allies than to the Revolution at home?

We will begin our reply to the questions propounded, by answering the ones presented last first. In this respect a peculiar coincidence, in the form of a newspaper expression published in the capital of one of the most powerful German states by the official organ of the working class, will serve as an effective illustration and source to throw light upon this subject. Just prior to the beginning of negotiations for an armistice and peace, questions similar to the ones just enumerated were the subject of much heated discussions and serious debates in the German press. The Socialist "Münchener Post" of October 10th, publishing a treatise from its Berlin correspondent, discussing the burning question "Who is responsible for Germany's latest and most all-embracing offer of peace?", writes:

"After Austria's note had been rejected, it was assumed that peace efforts would decline, although the 'high aim' of peace was not at all to be dropped, especially at a time when negotiations were progressing for the entrance of the Socialists into the capitalist government. The Social Democrats did not expect the Hertling crisis to bring peace directly, but that it would solely prepare the way for it. The thought was generally entertained that Germany would perform its metamorphosis into one of the most modern Democracies right under the eyes of the world, and thereby give concrete evidence of its willingness to conclude a democratic peace based upon mutual understanding. . . The expectations prevailed that the sight of this change in Germany's political atmosphere would also produce a change of opinion in the ranks of the enemy. However, it was estimated, that this would, under the most favorable conditions, require at least weeks or months. In the meantime, the national defense would have to be maintained, partly so the other side would appreciate the impossibility to achieve a decisive victory, and, secondly, to have the enemy see that it is no longer necessary to deal an annihilating blow to a Germany going through a fundamental process of reconstruction. In other words, the Socialists wanted to bring the war to an end—but gradually. The change that has since then taken place is, therefore, not at all to be attributed to the Socialists. . . Far from it that it came under the pressure of the Socialists—it came from the very opposite direction.

"This step was, consequently, not the effect of the fundamental love of peace inherent in Social-Democracy, but the result of a sudden recognition of the situation in entirely different circles. The new chancellor stated in his speech to the Reichstag that this step had been taken in conjunction with all influential factors. Of course, this was also previously stated, when new moves were to be undertaken; but then it was not the truth. However, at this time it is true; and, if we may so express ourselves, even truer than merely true. Relations have been shifted. The new government did nothing else but draw conclusions out of a given situation; more than that, it did not even draw these conclusions itself; they were offered from the outside."

4

From this report and more or less reliable opinion of the causes underlying the recent changes in the political makeup of Germany, the reader will glean that the peace propositions, and the radical steps which led up to them, were not at all evolved and introduced by the Social-Democrats, but rather the fruits of the labors and agitation carried on by the extreme conservative forces in the nation. Although the Social-Democrats were even under the empire slated for active participation in the government, the pressure of conditions was so great that this relatively radical move was considered too slow. So the theory of gradually democratizing Germany with the assistance or under the supervision of the Socialists was discarded, and the historic negotiations for an armistice and peace, with their famous endings, introduced and concluded.

From the above quoted version of the situation, this version receiving an authentic endorsement through its publication in the leading official organ of the Bavarian Social-Democracy, we can also glean that the majority of the Social-Democrats were up to a very recent date sailing "cheek-by-jowl" with the government of German Imperialism. At a whole, with the exception of a limited and to a large degree still incomplete and tactically defective propaganda carried on by the revolutionary Socialists of the Spartacus Group, the workers were quiet and doing their bit. At this juncture the, relatively considered, "victorious" offensive of the "gallant" German armies had just been concluded. And there was certainly very little spirit of rebellion in the German trenches, otherwise it would have asserted itself in the ignominious breakdown of this to human life so expensive slaughter.

Now the additional questions involuntarily crop up: Is it not highly remarkable and hardly conceivable for an army, resting in strategically excellent and almost impregnable positions all along the battlefront, positions achieved just recently through "glorious" victories over the enemy, to evacuate these positions or desert the trenches and wend their way home—returning as rabid Republicans or revolutionary Socialists? Furthermore, is it not highly original and thought-provoking for a model monarchical nation to metamorphose—"the rabble,' nobility, bourgeoisie, bureaucracy, Hindenburg and all—into a republican form of government almost over night? Does it not seem highly abnormal for a people to divest themselves so quickly of the feudal trappings and traditions centuries old, without giving preliminary indications of this change of attitude brewing within them? Does not the nature of these historic occurrences, and the acts so swiftly transpiring in this great world drama indicate or give rise to the not very pleasant suspicion that the Revolution, so speedily and almost automatically following upon the heels of the concluded armistice, has been prearranged or manufactured and foisted

5

upon the people from above? In order to intelligently appreciate this problem, and to be able to judge this complex situation scientifically and in its entirety, we must make a study of the basic and dynamic causes underlying and accountable for Germany's monumental military collapse.

II.

WE know, and believe it is unnecessary to dwell on this generally recognized proposition, that the prime cause of the Great War is to be found in the economic rivalry or industrial competition between the German Imperialists and those of the Allies. Consequently, as always, this bloody orgy was in the last analysis a struggle for economic supremacy; in this case it was a struggle raging around the proposition whether German or Allied Capital should dominate and reign supreme in the Balkans, Asia Minor and all other countries affected and made tributary by such a reign; furthermore, whether the Cape-Cairo railroad project would be interlocked or connected with that of the Bagdad Railway already under German supremacy or not, or whether this gigantic steel net which is to envelope Africa, Asia and Europe would partly function under the benevolent "protectorate" of the British, French and American syndicates; in short: whether the Imperialist interests, grouped around the banking houses of Berlin, would be powerful enough to assert themselves and develop their capitalist potentialities in the presence of the gigantic banking interests composing the Anglo-Saxon ring. A compromise was attempted in this connection and failed. The war, therefore, became inevitable and broke out. The Central Empires or the German Imperialists achieved some stupendous and telling victories on the battlefield. However, when actually within the reach of their much coveted prize, when within arm's length of Paris, the German offensive halted, and then, after some dickering and dallying, the German emissaries concluded the aforementioned armistice, the undefeated German batallions turned right about face, and, leaving, as a magnanimous victor, all their fruits of victory behind,—marched home. This act, at first so inexplicable, proclaimed the beginning of the end of the Great War, together with the absolute defeat and complete breakdown of German Imperialism. However, when contemplating these interesting events, we are again confronted by that insistent and tenacious query: What caused this ignominious and stupendous debacle of German Militarism, what superior forces accomplished the defeat of the undefeated troops of the Central Empires; what influential power or social element developed a superior might over the one wielded by the German military machine, and was thus able to prompt and compel this sudden and spectacular retreat, a retreat to which the one of Napoleon's legions seems pygmean?

When carefully studying the economic conditions and industrial history of Germany, we find that this country, before the war, had reached a wonderful and unparalleled degree of efficiency and productivity in certain basic industries; but also that it was a specialist in the production of certain commodities; furthermore, that due to geographical limits it had concentrated the major part of its economic resources in the development of these particular basic industries, and thus, due to this process of elimination and specialization, had gradually become everything but a country able to provide food, clothing and shelter for its people out of resources located within its own boundaries. We also find, when analyzing the industrial and social situation prevalent in the Central Empires during particularly the last six months of the war, that, especially from a standpoint of certain essential commodities in the departments of food stuffs, textiles, metals, etc., there existed a stringency or shortage which boded ill for the future economic intactness and tranquillity of these countries. However, there was not only an actual shortage in certain important necessities of warfare, but also a famine, affecting and embracing the people as a whole, and having its source in the general shortage of food, was threatening a country standing upon the threshold of a severe winter. Therefore, when the German troops launched the terrific offensive to penetrate the French lines, all Germany held its breath in keen anticipation and fearful anxiety, an anticipation and anxiety which grew out of the all determining problem—whether the troops would succeed to reach Paris and thus bring the war to a "victorious" end. A starving, undernourished but patriotic people, a people that had given millions of lives and willingly sacrificed a great part of the national vitality, had reached the last lap in the mad race for power, faithfully placing all their hopes of "victory" and deliverance from these hardships upon the outcome of this great drive. As the reader knows, the German offensive was successful, but did not reach Paris, nor did it end the war. Instead, the terrific aggressiveness manifested by the Germans in this drive served to whip on the mobilization of troops in America, with the result that ever greater numbers of Americans kept pouring into France; of course, thereby making the possibility for a decisive victory on the part of the Germans evermore hopeless. And, not to forget, all these manifestations were taking place and observed by the Germans in the shadow of an approaching winter with starvation for millions staring them into the face.

The last great German offensive failing to reach its object, and petering out into relatively insignificant gains; the flood of troops on the enemies' side menacingly continuing to rise; and the food, clothing and even supplies of ammunition getting shorter and more defective; these elements, although distinct in their manifestations, had in their effect upon the social life of Germany one thing in common: they brought home with an irrefutable and tragic force the terrible and to many unexpected message portending the crushing defeat and utter annihilation of German imperialistic aims and ideals. Of course, in this respect the ever growing economic disintegration in Germany was a far more important factor than the ever increasing military power of the Allies; because upon the intactness and healthy condition of German industry in general was predicated the intactness and healthy condition of Germany's military machine. Consequently, a collapse of Germany's economic anatomy did not only produce a similar collapse in the whole social life of the nation, but also manifested itself in that spectacular and ignominious breakdown of the German army and navy.

This economic debacle also definitely announced and convincingly emphasized the crushing defeat of German Imperialism by or suffered at the hands of the Anglo-Saxon oligarchy of finance. It furthermore irrefutably illustrates the economic superiority of Allied Capitalism, or, to be more explicit, Anglo-Saxon Imperialism over the Imperialism of the Teutons. Speaking broadly, the ample supply of food, clothing and other life necessities, in the hands of the Allies and mainly provided by the United States, was really the determining factor which won the war for Anglo-Saxon Imperialism, because it was just this lack of food, etc., that compelled the German Imperialists to capitulate. Primarily, therefore, the Great War has been a battle of wealth against wealth, with the logical result that the side possessing the greatest accumulation of industrial resources, i. e., the greatest economic power, won out.

Therefore, it is well to remember, when studying the Revolution, that its origin must be located and rests primarily in the economic collapse of Germany. Furthermore, that, due to this collapse, the bourgeoisie was compelled to adapt the political superstructure of Germany to meet the demands of the victors, demands which it knew would be insistently and arbitrarily made at the coming peace conference. In consequence, we must also bear in mind that the soldiers did not revolt against their superiors, but that the Revolution was directly or indirectly brought to them by their superiors. We must also not forget that the Revolution was enacted and in the majority of localities brought to a successful conclusion in a most orderly and remarkably well disciplined, organized manner; quietly but effectively running its course with the precision of a clock, thus serving as a most welcome and desirable supplement to the armistice agreement just concluded and the peace parleys visible on the horizon. Another peculiarity of the Revolution, one for which no precedent can be found in similar revolutionary epochs, is presented in the attitude of the former officials and government employees; an attitude which manifested itself in a surprising policy of non-resistance to and acceptance of the authority of the Revolution, and which reached its culmination when even the generals of imperial Germany, including the national idol Hindenburg and the elite of the nobility, without much ado, renounced their loyalty to the Empire and swore allegiance to the Republic. Strangely, in this former stronghold of monarchy and feudal prerogatives, there was little or no protest to be noticed from loyal regiments generally recruited from relatively backward agrarian districts; no serious fighting or counterstrokes engaged in by the royalists; at a whole, no vigorous indications of dissatisfaction or protest to be noticed on the part of the stand-pat conservative elements forming not a small fraction of the German populace.

The above social symptoms and historic manifestations compel us, although unwillingly, to conclude with ever greater conviction that the Revolution in Germany was inaugurated primarily upon the initiative and under the tentative but forceful guidance of the ruling classes. To illustrate, if the Revolution were at its inception a class-conscious proletarian revolution, it would immediately have repudiated and ousted the coterie of Social Patriots even at this writing at the head of the German government, and supported the policies, if not of the Spartacus Group, then at least of the Independent Socialists. As we know, the German workers did neither; they gave and are giving their full support to the Majority Social-Democrats, to men who see in the inauguration of the Bourgeois Republic a highly revolutionary act. And to the average German worker, the establishment of political Democracy will mean and undoubtedly is a great step forward.

III.

AS the ultimate success of the Socialist movement, different from any other movement, is measured by the quality or degree of class-consciousness inherent in it, it will probably be of interest to note the strength of the so-called Social Patriots and the astonishing weakness of the class-conscious Socialists manifested in the election returns of the delegates to the National Soldiers' and Workingmen's Congress which recently convened in Berlin. If these returns can at all be considered a basis for the quality or character of the Socialist conception or class-consciousness prevalent amongst the German workers, and we cannot see why they should not furnish a most classical criterion, then the following observations and rather disconnected deductions are offered for consideration:

1. On December 17, the first Soldiers' and Workingmen's Congress, composed of 450 delegates from all over Germany,

assembled in the building formerly occupied by the Prussian Diet in Berlin and went into session.

2. As this congress was exclusively made up of members of the proletariat, a unified and sharp class attitude on all questions coming before it for discussion was to be expected—an attitude breaking once and for all with the spirit of harmony and fraternity preached and practised by the Majority Socialists during the four years of the war. Of course, this revolutionary attitude was only to be expected, if the rank and file of the German workers, reflected in the 450 assembled delegates, were constituted of a vastly different material than that exhibited by the overwhelming majority of their leaders prior to and during the war. That this revolutionary spirit in the intellectual make-up and tactical attitude would prevail and flagrantly manifest itself amongst the German proletariat, the recognized Bolshevist journals in America did not even consider worthy of questioning. To "The Revolutionary Age," A Chronicle and Interpretation of Events in Europe, of December 7th, in an article captioned "The Stranglers of Socialism?", the situation presented itself as follows:

Just prior to the revolution, it was a race between armistice and the revolution, between Marshal Foch and Karl Liebknecht. The Revolution and Liebknecht conquered. But it was a conquest that marked simply the first stage of the Revolution; the next necessary conquest, which alone will make the Revolution a real revolution, is the conquest of Capitalism and Imperialism, the establishment of a Socialist proletarian government.

In an article "Reconstruction in Germany," appearing a week later in the same organ which triumphantly had announced Liebknecht's and the Revolution's victory over Foch and armistice, we read the following compilation of problems confronting the German workers:

The problem of reconstruction which the German proletariat must tackle is the same as the problem of the proletariat of France, Belgium, Great Britain and Italy, enormously complicated by military disaster and the collapse of the power of German Capitalism for successful imperialistic competition.

Revolutionary Socialism in Germany insists that real reconstruction is possible only through Socialism, by means of conquest of power by the proletariat. The whole system of Capitalism and Imperialism comprised in the old German system must be destroyed; reconstruction must proceed without paying the tribute of profit to the capitalist class, without reconstruction being limited and stultified by the profit system. The reconstruction of a new society, the real healing of the wounds of the war, the protection of the proletariat against oppression and new wars, is not possible while Capitalism and Imperialism persist in Germany.

Revolutionary Socialism in Germany, moreover, realizes that indemnities would complicate the problem of reconstruction in Germany, and would not measurably ease the burdens and facilitate the process of real reconstruction for the proletariat of Belgium, Great Britain, France and Italy. Revolutionary Socialism, accordingly, struggles for the proletarian revolution in Germany as the climax of the proletarian revolution in

10

Russia, and equally struggles for the proletarian revolution in the rest of Europe, since only by the general overthrow of Capitalism and the general dictatorship of the proletariat can reconstruction proceed on a basis of Socialism, of healing the wounds of labor, and not of capital. Revolutionary Socialism strives for an alliance with Soviet Russia and with revolutionary Socialism in all European countries.

This is not an attempt to shift the burden—that is the policy of Capitalism in Germany, not of revolutionary Socialism—since the overthrow of Capitalism will facilitate real reconstruction and benefit equally the proletariat everywhere.

Moderate Socialism in Germany, in policy and as represented in the bourgeois-"Socialist" Government, refuses to accept the overthrow of capitalist supremacy as the necessary preliminary to real reconstruction. "The Berlin Bourse," says a press report, "and banking and industrial circles do not expect the immediate enactment of radical measures. The impression prevails that the Ebert-Haase Government is convinced that the present political and economic situation is inauspicious."

In another article entitled "The Revolution in Germany," originally published in the Call Magazine, of November 17, 1918, Ludwig Lore sums up the situation as follows:

It is true, hunger and war-weariness are the forces that are driving its engines. But, far from floundering blindly about, it is steering directly forward to its ultimate destination, held true to its course by the revolutionary understanding of the masses. The theoretical Marxian training that the German movement gave to its rank and file in the past—the understanding, that, in spite of all political accomplishments, the complete overthrow of capitalism alone can achieve the liberation of the working class from exploitation, will save the social revolution in Germany from many bitter and costly mistakes. With a clearness and inflexibility of purpose that recalls the German movement under August Bebel and Wilhelm Liebknecht, it has gone through three different phases of development within two short weeks of time—from a bourgeois ministry, with the co-operation of three social patriots, to a coalition ministry of Socialists and Liberals, under Socialist domination, to a Socialist ministry representing all wings of the Socialist movement, under the direct control of the Soldiers' and Workmen's Councils.

The revolution in Germany still is developing, and, if the future realizes present promises, will ultimately place the revolutionary elements of the German Social Democratic movement where they belong—at the helm of the German Socialist republic.

After a perusal of the situation and the three versions presented above, the following questions automatically take on shape and form: What is the actual strength of revolutionary Socialism in Germany, especially when compared with that of moderate Socialism? Has the German working class, a working class that for four years almost to a man supported the Majority Socialists, become revolutionary and theoretically enlightened over night; or is the theory of Ludwig Lore correct, did these workers, the offsprings of the movement of Bebel and Liebknecht, only place their theoretical clarity and revolutionary training in cold storage for four years, in order to redeem it at this opportune moment for utilization in the cause of the German Socialist Republic? Did this theoretical Marxian training that the German movement gave to its rank and file in the past—the under-

11

standing that, in spite of all political accomplishments, the complete overthrow of Capitalism alone can achieve the liberation of the working class from exploitation—actually rest in some intellectual safe deposit vault during all the momentous and vital episodes in the political life of Germany? Was the vehement and at times bitter condemnation of the German Social-Democracy, of which millions of German workers with the Marxian training also form an incidental part—that Social-Democracy whose previous methods and tactics were so forcefully placed into the pillory by the "N. Y. Volkszeitung"—all a mistake, and are we, now that the big slaughter is over, to be waited on again with that in "bygone days" so judiciously circulated theory lauding German Socialist efficiency, discipline, three million votes and 110 representatives; in other words, is the importation of Social-Democratic canned goods to be resumed? Yes, gentlemen of the Ultra-Left Wing in the S. P., was it all a mistake? Is the rank and file of the German proletariat so revolutionary, as implied by the above quoted three versions, to be ready to repudiate or ostracize its Social Patriots? Has this working class of the August days of 1914 become trained and class-conscious in the school of hard knocks; are the majority of the workers in sympathy with the principles of revolutionary Socialism as symbolized by the Spartacus Group? Is it a fact that the German soldiers, who in October were still vigorously prosecuting an offensive against Paris, who had to be ordered out of the trenches, have during this short period been revolutionized in the interests of international Socialism? Not only is it a fact, but is such a fundamental intellectual revolution realizable, yes possible, in such a short lapse of time? Let documentary evidence in the form of a manifesto issued by the Social-Democratic Party of Germany and the results of the aforementioned elections to the National Soldiers' and Workingmen's Congress answer these so interesting and vital questions. Incidentally, when perusing the two quotations from "The Revolutionary Age," we also suggest a re-reading of the article from the "Münchener Post," published in the first part of this essay, and showing that the so-called race between Marshal Foch and Karl Liebknecht may have originated in the phantasy of the editorial scribe of this "Chronicle and Interpretation of Events in Europe," but in actuality existed only in an adaptation of German institutions by the German Imperialists—to meet the requirements of the terms in the armistice of Marshal Foch.

3. The Social-Democratic Party of Germany in a manifesto entitled "An Appeal to Reason," published in the "Dresdener Volkszeitung" on November 6th, expresses the following interesting versions and criticisms of the turbulent conditions, versions and criticisms, it must be emphasized, upon which the delegates to the Soldiers' and Workingmen's Congress were

subsequently elected, and versions and criticisms with which, alas, the majority of the German proletariat seems to be heartily in accord:

THE SOCIAL-DEMOCRATIC PARTY TO THE WORKING PEOPLE.

Workingmen and Workingwomen:

The dreadful slaughter is going to an end; there can be no thought of continuing it.

Peace is coming. It places the working class before the most difficult *economic and political tasks.*

Politically the problem will be to insure and develop the democratic liberty attained. Those, who through their disastrous politics are guilty of the misery and unhappiness of our people, must disappear from their places.

The steps necessary for this have been instituted; they shall halt before no one, high as his position may be.

Economically the task is to provide subsistence for the people, and to perform the transformation to a state of peace in such a manner, *so that no one need starve.* For this purpose the most efficient organization of employment agencies, and a sufficient support for the unemployed is necessary. These duties can, however, impossibly be realized, if chaos prevails.

If *riots* develop, then the already inadequate machinery for the provision of foodstuffs *will entirely break down*, the working population will be **surrendered** to a death of *starvation*, while the possessing layers in society will still be able to help themselves. This also occurred in Russia and not even the methods of force employed by Bolshevism were able to alter anything thereon.

If riots originate, then additional plants will have to close down, and it will not be possible to support the enormous army of unemployed. For the returning comrades from the battlefield there will be no work to find and they will, as far as they can, attempt to help themselves upon their own account. This will lead to new inner struggles, which will have additional *immeasurable misery* following in their wake.

Can and shall, therefore, the working class *abandon any of its demands* which it must place in the interests of its future political and industrial liberty? We say—no! It would rather *take the hardest consequences to its members upon itself!*

The tremendous sacrifices, which the working people have made in this war, entitle them to the most far-reaching demands. Their realization produces the preliminary requirements for Socialism. However, this gigantic reconstruction of society can not be completed in days and weeks; for this task much *struggle* and *labor* will yet be required.

We will not lose sight of our aims; from our demands we will not surrender one! However, the means, as long as this is at all possible, we shall so select, so the working class will not cut into its own flesh.

We are a power, if we are united; let us employ this power! However, let us beware of irresponsibly and without necessity calling forth a chaos, through which our antagonists, but *also we will have to suffer most severely.*

Therefore we address to you the following appeal: Join in masses the political organization of the Social-Democracy, join the modern, free trades unions (modernen, freien Gewerkschaften)! In these organizations you can be the forward pushing element. But beware of splits and disintegration, of a warfare amongst brothers, and of the advice of irresponsible elements, who desire to mislead you into a senseless struggle against your own interests. Do not follow the battlecries of *small groups and unknown demagogues.* If the workers run hither and thither, or even begin to *tear themselves to pieces*, nothing substantial can be gained therefrom, but only indescribable disaster.

You and your children are at stake! Therefore, once more: Preserve unity, presence of mind, and the discipline of the organization. No Russian conditions, but the whole in closed ranks forward towards the aims of Democracy and Socialism.

THE EXECUTIVE COMMITTEE OF THE SOCIAL-DEMOCRATIC PARTY OF GERMANY.

4. We will now let the reports of the aforementioned elections also assist in answering some of the above propounded questions. These reports show that the by far vast majority of the 450 delegates constituting the Soldiers' and Workingmen's Congress belonged to and was made up of sympathizers with the Majority Socialists; also that the Independent Socialists or Kautsky-Haase adherents exercised a relatively small influence, voting, as for instance on the question of calling a National Constituent Assembly, repeatedly with the Majority Socialists against the already insignificant and surprisingly weak minority representing and expressing the revolutionary concepts of the Spartacus Group.

5. We are now also compelled to admit that the Soldiers' and Workingmen's Congress, during its short but agitated session in Berlin, did not only emphatically repudiate Liebknecht and the principles of his group, by turning down the Spartacides' proposition to reject the motion for a National Constitutional Convention and solely work for a dictatorship of the proletariat, but furthermore proclaimed its fealty to Opportunism by also giving Liebknecht and German Bolshevism a black eye in the form of: First, electing one Robert Leinert, a well known member of the Social Patriots and one of the slimiest labor fakirs in Germany, to the permanent chairmanship of the Congress; and secondly, by adopting, with a vote of 200 against 40, a motion to set January 19th as the date for the national elections to the Constitutional Convention.

From the evidence submitted in the six illustrations, although at times inadequate and disconnected, also from the proceedings of the above cited congress, we can readily surmise that the spirit and intellectual make-up of the German workers may be defined as everything but revolutionary; of course, estimating the term revolutionary to be identical with a class-conscious, scientific conception of Socialism. It is a spirit which has been broken or at least radically influenced by many years of suffering, and which is now completely crushed by the spectacular economic catastrophe sweeping over the fatherland. It seems that these workers have but one desire, one great longing for—food, clothing, shelter and tranquillity. For these essentials of life they will resort to and sacrifice anything. The proletarian revolution, were it to be inaugurated, would be doomed to a hopeless defeat, because of its inability, its absolute economic

14

unpreparedness, to provide food, clothing and shelter to starving Germany.

Economic security of life! Who has the necessities so imperative to satisfy these elementary demands? That is the burning question asked daily by the suffering German populace, and as it is propounded, instinctively, the eyes of the anxious interrogator turn towards the west and rest upon the boundless natural resources of America. Yes, although it seems paradoxical and a strange irony of fate, to well stocked and abundantly provisioned America starving, helpless and industrially ruined Central Europe looks and is dependent upon for help. The United States, being economically the most powerful, will, therefore, also be the most influential factor at the approaching Peace Conference; and whatever this conference, under the tentative guidance or economic iron heel of the U. S. dictates, Germany and her brothers in misfortune will be compelled to accept, *because an economically crippled and disorganized nation, whose population is practically upon the brink of starvation, has no choice.*

For a social revolution, no moment is more inopportune than the present in Germany. Anglo-Saxon Imperialism in possession of her forts, fleet, most efficient military equipment and a vital part of her rolling stock; the population starving, freezing and a severe winter before them; furthermore, millions of men returning home crippled and enervated by years of barbaric carnage; under such ungratifying, yes, tragic conditions, the people will and can harbor only one fond desire, and that is not revolution but—relief! To get this relief or make it possible, certain radical changes and conditions had to be complied with —the abolition of monarchy and the inauguration of the Republic belonged to them. Not only were these qualifications for relief, but they were the fundamental condition for a rapprochement, the basis for a possibility of negotiations between the Allies and Germany. German Imperialism, dancing upon an industrial and social volcano, knowing that a speedy capitulation was a matter of self-preservation; also knowing that, if entering the peace negotiations as a Republic, it would save itself quite a few galling humiliations, remove the source of a popular and fertile antipathy and regain part of the good-will and confidence sacrificed during the war, therefore, sought to expel as speedily as possible the feudal remnants from its system, and thus became the bitter foe of monarchical government. In other words, as soon as the German bourgeoisie noted and became conscious of its economic breakdown; perceived its helpless state and the possibility of victory forever removed out of its reach; found itself utterly at the mercy of its foes, what was there more logical for this class-conscious coterie of surplus-value spongers to do than to work for the best possible or the most profitable terms obtainable under this gigantic receivership? The deposition of the

15

Kaiser and other members of the governing fraternity throughout Germany and Austria-Hungary was the first move in this direction; the launching of a republican form of government signifies the second act of preparation for the great reunion—the Peace Conference. When viewed from this angle we must admit that the German Revolution did breathe a spirit of class-consciousness, but primarily of the defeated bourgeoisie—not the proletariat.

IV.

WHEN taking the proceedings of and the general spirit dominant and displayed at the National Conference of the Soldiers' and Workingmen's Councils as a criterion for our deductions, we are compelled to conclude that Revisionism and not Socialism, the desire for political Democracy and not the Industrial Republic reigned supreme at this historic gathering. If this representative assembly of workers from every part of Germany can be considered a yardstick with which to measure the psychology and general ideology, i. e., with which to determine the theoretical and tactical degree of class-consciousness prevalent in the German proletariat, then we are again, much to our regret, forced to admit that a conference controlled and veritably swamped with delegates, pledged to support the official policy of the Majority Socialists, i. e., the so pliable policy of Revisionism, against the proletarian Internationalism of the Spartacus Group; that a conference even fearing to admit the official Russian delegation as fraternal delegates—thus committing an unforgiveable and most flagrant act of betrayal of international solidarity in general and the struggling Russian Revolution in particular; that a conference electing a Robert Leinert as its permanent chairman, a man who personifies the worst and most corrupted phases of an Opportunism audaciously buccaneering under the flag of Socialism, may reflect and signify everything and anything but a sound class-conscious theoretical and tactical training and understanding on the part of the German workers; such a conference denotes everything and anything on the part of the same proletarians, but the competence to participate consciously and intelligently in the revolutionary class struggle raging in society; and finally, when viewed from a revolutionary class position, this exhibition also betrays a total lack of judgment appertaining to current events and exigencies on the part of the German working class as a class. To expect workers, who gave birth to such a conference, to vigorously prosecute or carry on the struggle for the social revolution, to expect them to act in a class-conscious manner, is to expect the impossible—is to anticipate a wonder.

The present conduct of the majority of German workers, manifesting itself in their loyalty to and support of the principles of Opportunism, is fully in accord with the many years of training received in these principles and tactics through the regular "edu-

16

cational" institutions of the party. We presume that Ludwig Lore is referring to this exquisite training, when he emphasizes "the theoretical Marxian training that the German movement gave to its rank and file in the past." The attitude of the Social-Democratic party of Germany was always one outspokenly "practical and reformistic": It was an attitude primarily evolved not by a party of Socialism, but one developed by an organization pledged to an immediate programme of political democratic reform. Therefore, the most revolutionary plank in its programme of political reforms was the one demanding the Republic. For decades the party had worked "successfully" along the lines of palliation, and persistently and consistently advocated the removal and abolition of certain feudal prerogatives so drastically symbolized by certain antiquated election laws and political institutions in Germany. Just as the realization of the Industrial Republic presented itself only as a fascinating Fata Morgana with which to hypnotize the masses to the Revisionists, so also the abolition of the monarchy and the introduction of the Republic became to be gradually regarded by them as a highly improbable and colossally revolutionary act. Gradually, Socialism, as the ultimate aim of the German Social-Democracy, was thrust into obscurity and made way for the "revolutionary" goal proclaiming the Republic; until, slowly but surely, the demand for the Republic also began to grow unpopular, and was beginning to be gently relegated into oblivion, the practical politicians placing certain "radical" demands for a "reconstruction" of the political machinery upon which the imperial government was based in its place,—when, relatively considered, like a bolt out of a clear sky, the crash came, giving birth to the Republic; and, as will be readily understood from the foregoing, not so much due to the republican potentialities working from within, but the threatening pressure asserting itself from without.

The reader is now cautioned against confounding the ideology of the average American or English worker with the social vision of the German proletarian. Such a comparison may be permissible, but will also convincingly show the great gulf which separates these two proletarian psychologies—a gulf whose origin is to be located in the two distinctly different routes taken by industrial and political development in the countries cited. Germany is undoubtedly, with the United States and England, one of the most highly developed industrial countries in the world. Germany enjoys all the benefits accruing from a practically fullfledged capitalist development. However, Germany's economic climb was performed under entirely different historic conditions than that of, let us say, other classical national units of Capitalism, and has been accomplished to a large degree in the last half of the Nineteenth Century. The fact must not be lost sight of, particularly when studying and judging the political atmosphere

17

and institutions of the country, that Germany as a national entity or political unit is not even fifty years old; furthermore, that the unification of Germany, and the economic development projecting and finally compelling such a political unity, unlike the industrial and political process of evolution and unification as prevailed in England, France and the United States, was repeatedly obstructed, stunted and postponed by a chain of wars, amongst them the Thirty and Seven-Years' Wars, in whose wake followed periods of devastation, disintegration and decadence as yet unparalleled in the annals of history. While England, France and "isolated and secluded" America were adapting their political institutions to meet the constantly changing economic requirements, i. e., accomplishing their emancipation from Feudalism via the bourgeois revolution, the German states were time and time again thrown back into a hopeless state of chaos and utter economic ruin. These abnormalities, upon whose origin and effects we cannot dwell here, abnormalities, of course, only when compared with the process of social evolution during the same period in other countries, were the principal factors, the basic cause, which delayed the arrival of the bourgeois republic in Germany, and also encourged the cultivation of a reactionary psychology amongst the people necessarily resulting from social and political institutions resting upon feudal soil. Only these historical peculiarities and abnormal manifestations in the industrial history of that country will explain the tenacious existence of feudal political institutions, and all the medieval social garnishings accompanying them, side by side with a vigorous and efficient system of capitalist production up to the recent outbreak; they will also explain the peculiar and distinctly German conditions under which the German Socialist movement had to operate; backward conditions so intelligently appraised and appreciated by Wilhelm Liebknecht, when stating in his "No Compromise etc.," page 14:

In addition to that we must take into consideration the political backwardness of the bourgeoisie in Germany, which is the cause of the fact that there does not exist here a really liberal party, to say nothing of a democratic party. This fact has this as its natural results: that the honestly liberal and democratic elements of the bourgeoisie gravitate more and more towards the side of the Social-Democracy as the only party which is fighting for democratic principles in Germany. But these democratic elements do not thereby become Socialists, though many believe they are Socialists. In short, we have now in Germany a phenomenon which has been observable in France for half a century and longer, and which has contributed much to the confusion of party relations in France, viz.: that a part of the radical bourgeoisie rallies around the Socialist flag without understanding the nature of socialism. This political socialism, which in fact is only philanthropic humanitarian radicalism, has retarded the development of socialism in France exceedingly. It has diluted and blurred the principles and weakened the socialist party because it brought into it troops upon which no reliance could be placed in the decisive moment.

Therefore, to a people only shortly but so fundamentally

18

revolutionized by a gigantic industrial revolution, however, born
and cultivated in a political and social atmosphere exhaling the
spirit of feudal prerogatives and a capitalist oligarchy in the making, an oligarchy threatening to foist an unprecedented industrial
slavery upon them, to such a people Democracy is a vital demand
of the hour, yes—a revolutionary demand, and, consequently, every
Democrat a revolutionist. And to Socialists, who conceived in a
Wm. Jennings Bryan and Samuel Gompers comrades, Democracy
and the realization of the Republic will be undoubtedly considered a great revolutionary agent and achievement. And that the
inauguration of political Democracy will also have a clarifying
effect upon the Socialist movement of Germany we must admit,
when we perceive the corrupting and confusing influence which
the reactionary political situation exercised upon the development of the Social-Democratic Party. Wm. Liebknecht, writing
on page 15 in the same pamphlet cited above, depicts the situation, and the problems resulting therefrom, as follows:

The disappearance of fear and aversion to us in political circles of
course brings political elements into our ranks. As long as this takes
place on a small scale it causes no apprehension because the political
elements are outnumbered by the proletarian elements and are gradually
assimilated. But it is a different thing if the political elements in the party
become so numerous and influential that their assimilation becomes
difficult and even the danger arises that the proletarian socialist element
will be crowded to the rear. This danger of politicalization threatens the
German Social Democracy from two sources *on account of the backwardness of our bourgeoisie.* First, the democratic elements of the bourgeoisie,
which find no political satisfaction in their own class, flow to us in greater
numbers than in countries with a normally developed bourgeoisie; second,
the bureaucratic, though capitalistic, spirit of our governments tends towards a state socialism which, in fact, is only state capitalism, but which
is dazzling and misleading for those who are easily deceived by external
similarities and catch words. The German, or more accurately the Prussian, state socialism whose ideal is a military, landlord and police state,
hates democracy above everything else.

Taking the analysis and characterization of the situation in
Germany presented in the foregoing as a criterion, an analysis
and characterization which we claim to be fully in accord with
historic facts and which can be amply supported with documentary and scientific evidence, how, under such conditions certain
Socialists can and will persist in interpreting the German Revolution as a social revolution, and will, in the face of all historic
and current evidence to the contrary, persist in proclaiming the
bourgeois Republic of Germany a Socialist Republic, is something
the writer cannot explain through any other but the purely sentimental axiom making "the wish father to the thought." That
there is a revolutionary element, recently organized in the Communist Labor Party, in Germany, we know. We also know,
however, that this element, finding theoretical expression in the
writings of Karl Liebknecht, Rosa Luxemburg, Franz Mehring
and others, is not at all a unit with reference to the tactical pro-

gramme and requirements imperative for a clear cut revolutionary party of Socialism in a country like Germany; we furthermore know, that this young political movement of revolutionary Socialism is still deficient and untrained in the destructive and constructive functions allotted by historical development to Socialist Industrial Unionism in this great struggle of the workers for industrial emancipation; and, finally, without at all desiring to detract from the significance of the Communist Labor Party in the political life of Germany, we also know that the popularity of the erstwhile Spartacus Group or some of its prominent adherents in America is not at all in proportion to its actual strength and popularity amongst the rank and file of the German working class. How otherwise can the so discouraging and crushing defeat of the candidates of the Spartacides, standing for election to the National Soldiers' and Workingmen's Congress, be explained?

The overwhelming defeat of the revolutionary Socialists at the recent elections, also the repudiation of their principles and tactics by the National Soldiers' and Workingmen's Congress, an assembly, as has been already emphasized before, mainly, if not solely, elected by members of the *organized* proletariat, carries to us another significant message, a message which points out an inherent weakness in the economic organization of the German proletariat, a weakness, however, easily explainable after reading the above, but nevertheless a weakness. The message contained in the above events announces that the Majority Socialists under the leadership of Carl Legien are still in supreme control of the numerically so powerful German trades union movement. It seems that, with the exception of a few local organizations in Berlin, Hamburg and other industrial centres, the economic organizations of the workers, these so all important and indispensable levers of the proletarian revolution, are still in the hands of and under the corrupting and devitalizing influence of Opportunism and the so-called Socialists of the majority party. The task of revolutionizing the German workers, a slow and tedious task, we know, must set in here. The millions of organized workers, members of the "Socialist" Freien Gewerkschaften, must first be captured for revolutionary Socialism, before we can consistently look in Germany for the Industrial Republic. This is the greatest task before the Communist Labor Party of Germany; will the organization measure up to the requirements of the hour?

Therefore, to sum up: With the psychology of Opportunism dominating the overwhelming majority of the German workers; with these principles and those of a victorious Democracy animating and vitalizing the war-weary and starving workers, the possibility for a period of social revolution, and for the Industrial Republic in Germany is removed out of the immediate vision—

out of the pale of the realizable. However, not only is the vast majority of German workers, due to social forces we have sufficiently dwelt upon, absolutely incompetent and unprepared to appreciate the scope and social significance of revolutionary Socialism; not only is it unconscious of its social position and historic function as a class; and, therefore, not only is this vast and pliable majority the willing instrument of Opportunism on the political field; but, due to this very absence of class-consciousness, its highly centralized and, in many cases industrial organizations on the economic field have been paralyzed, veritably struck with impotence, and can not take, hold and operate the social instruments of production in the interests of the Industrial Republic. These workers cannot primarily take, hold and operate through their respective organizations the industries and land, because they are not ripe for socialization, but solely because their collective will, their social desire as a majority class, has not been developed and made conscious of the necessity for such a basic economic revolution. Here we also have a concrete historical manifestation lucidly illustrating the irrefutable contention of Marxism: that the revolutionary vitality and power of organizations or social layers are not fundamentally reared and developed by the numbers affiliated with and the specific organic structure upon which a movement rests, but by the degree of class-consciousness inherent in its members—a class-consciousness, which, as it grows, will again react upon and reflect itself in the structure and general character of the institutions and organizations projected and developed by the various classes in a given society.

Furthermore, the present interesting stages in the development of the Socialist movement also drastically exhibit the fallacy of the propositions of drilling and educating the workers in one set of principles for years and then expecting the impossible to become possible, namely—the workers to repudiate these principles over night. They convincingly attest that you cannot teach the workers Opportunism in its classical form in times of peace, and expect them to miraculously metamorphose into revolutionists in times of war; that the principles and tactics of a movement, taking on powerful organized forms, are bound to be effective to the degree that they are organized to meet in line with certain historic requirements; and that, therefore, a movement like the German Social-Democracy, primarily organized to obtain immediate palliation in the shape of social and political reforms for the workers, and whose great ultimate objective rested in the overthrow of monarchy or the inauguration of political Democracy, was bound to function properly and successfully in a purely political revolution like the one just witnessed, but was also bound to refuse to function or dismally collapse in a revolution projecting Industrial Democracy as its goal.

21

That Dictatorship of the Proletariat

SINCE the establishment of the Political Dictatorship of the Bolsheviki in Russia, the slogan, calling for a Dictatorship of the Proletariat in other countries, has grown to be quite popular and is steadily increasing in volume. With reference to Russia, we presume, it is unnecessary to emphasize that the Dictatorship of Bolshevism cannot be identified and should not be considered synonymous with the establishment of Socialism in that country. This is due to certain historic peculiarities which, we believe, we need not dwell upon here. However, as a preliminary constructive force for the development of a class-conscious proletarian movement in Russia; and as a highly conducive element for the elimination of all vestiges of Feudalism, Bolshevism cannot be too highly estimated. In this connection, the Dictatorship of Bolshevism in Russia may also be termed and considered the dictatorship of the *developing* class-consciousness in the proletariat in particular and the oppressed classes in general of that country. How long Bolshevism will be able to retain the political supremacy, taking the complete victory of Anglo-Saxon Imperialism over Germany, and the economic impotence of the recently revolutionized and democratized German Republic as a guiding force, we cannot foretell. However, we are certain that even the political defeat or deposition of Bolshevism by Anglo-Saxon Imperialism can only redound to the ultimate benefit of the proletarian movement in Russia.

Taking the situation in Germany as a basis for contemplation along the same lines, we are compelled to draw entirely different conclusions. Because, where a pure or sole Dictatorship of the Proletariat in Russia is an absolute impossibility, owing to the backwardness of industrial development in that country, i. e., *owing to the absence of the proletariat as the majority class in the population*, a Dictatorship of the Proletariat in Germany is absolutely possible and in line with the social requirements flowing from the economic conditions of that country. However, when granting the possibility and necessity for the establishment of the Industrial Republic in Germany through the political Dictatorship of the Proletariat, we also are quite able to differentiate between what is necessary and that which is possible at the present time.

We know that Germany, due to certain abnormal phases in her development, although a classical country of Capitalism, has,

22

up to the inception of the Revolution, been a country loaded down with feudal prerogatives and institutions, i. e., socially "blessed" and obstructed with the remnants of an economic system from which it had completely emancipated itself. We are also aware that these feudal legacies have been a great negative element and hindrance in the propaganda and educational work of the Socialist movement of Germany. Due to the crying necessity of first democratizing Germany, the Socialist movement has in the past been mainly occupied with the demand and propaganda for the bourgeois Republic in Germany. Of course, a Socialist Party, considering this as its most immediate revolutionary object in its every day struggles, will attract quite a large element sympathetic to republican ideas, *but not necessarily sympathetic to or even possessing a smattering of Socialism.* Since the outbreak of the Revolution, the effects of this propaganda have been visibly felt and are playing quite an important role in the present agitated political life in Germany They have produced the interesting though ungratifying paradox of a large mass of the workers, although living in a highly centralized capitalist country, a country industrially rotten ripe for Socialism on the one hand, being absolutely unfamiliar with the historic function of the Socialist movement on the other. This large and overwhelming majority of proletarians supports the Opportunists organized in the Social Democratic Party, because these Opportunists seem to be realizing those very demands for which the *official* Social Democratic Party has for years been carrying on a most systematic and vigorous propaganda; a propaganda also in the past supported by the men to-day in the Independent Social Democratic Party, and even by quite a few members of the Spartacus Group. In consequence, with the Republic practically insured in Germany, the majority of workers, seeing in this political institution the realization of their fondest and most revolutionary aspirations, cannot, for the time at least, conceive and grasp in their victorious elation the urgent necessity for more fundamental and class-conscious changes. That is the basic reason why the Majority Socialists are in absolute control of the situation, *and can base their control upon the support of the majority in the working class. A Dictatorship of the Proletariat, as it manifests itself in the government of Ebert and consorts, can, therefore, be nothing else but a Dictatorship of Opportunism.*

Before the Dictatorship of the Proletariat in Germany, and for that matter in all classical countries of Capitalism, will and can be synonymous with the Dictatorship of revolutionary Socialism, the proletariat must be permeated with and adhere to the principles of uncompromising and scientific Marxism. *It is absurd to expect a proletariat like the German to give birth to any other kind of a dictatorship than it did.*

At present, the economic organizations of the German work-

23

ers are absolutely controlled by the Opportunists, therefore, *the economic power of the proletariat, organized at the point of production,* is pledged to and can be exploited by not the revolutionary demands of the Spartacides, but the usual reformistic aspirations of the Opportunists. To change the attitude of these millions of workers will require quite some expenditure of energy in the line of consistent education and also time. Of course, the limitations and basic deficiency inherent in mere political Democracy will also make themselves felt before long. The dissatisfaction growing out of the recognition of this fact, coupled with the substantial education disseminated by revolutionary Socialists, will then establish the basis for a class-conscious movement in Germany. And only out of such a movement can the power necessary for the wielding of a *powerful* Dictatorship of the Proletariat be developed. Before this great revolution in the theoretical and tactical concepts of the German workers has taken place, it would be fool-hardy to expect any genuine and fundamental revolution in the interests of the Socialist Republic in that country.

Therefore, we can greet with real satisfaction the segregation of Socialist forces in Germany. At present we are informed that the members of the Spartacus Group have finally decided to organize themselves into a regular political party under the name of The Communist Labor Party. At the Convention that gave birth to this new organization, the proposition was formulated that "no honest proletarian can have anything to do with the Independent Socialists." We presume that the members of the Communist Labor Party wished to affirm that no class-conscious proletarian can have anything to do with any other organization but the Communist Labor Party, *an attitude which is similar, if not identical, with the one taken by the Socialist Labor Party of America.*

As stated before, this clearing of the ground and closer drawing of the lines along certain fundamental principles is bound to redound advantageously to the establishment of clarity in the Socialist movement of Germany. We can also greet these changes as a systematic segregation of the different elements in the working class, and as the collapse of that plastic and insipid policy of "unity at all costs."

The class-conscious element in the German working class, under the leadership of Rosa Luxemburg, Franz Mehring, Karl Liebknecht and others, has at last established a party of Socialism firmly repudiating reform, and proclaiming the overthrow of Capitalism and the establishment of the Industrial Republic as its only immediate and ultimate demand. In America we have quite a large minority in the Socialist Party mouthing and demanding the Dictatorship of the Proletariat for Germany and other countries. In many respects, these American Bolshevists or adherents of Liebknecht are, as it is generally the case, more revolutionary than their masters. The question which we now present to them is, whether they will also follow the footsteps of the revolutionary Socialists in Germany, leave the more than opportunistic Socialist Party, and join the Socialist Labor Party—a party which N. Lenine, according to an article published and circulated by the Socialist Propaganda League, defines as harboring the real Internationalists. Will the ultra-revolutionary Left-Wingers in the so-called Socialist Party cut loose from this corrupted organism, will they possess enough integrity of principles to once and for all divorce themselves from an organization with which they have nothing in common, follow the policy of Liebknecht and his comrades and join an organization that really voices the revolutionary demands of the hour? By the attitude which they take on this question the sincerity and significance of the members, constituting the Left Wing in the Socialist Party, will be measured. If Germany is ripe for a Communist Labor Party, and if the revolutionary Socialists in that country have recognized the necessity of expressing their principles through a distinct political party of Socialism, then the Socialist Movement in the United States is certainly ripe for the Socialist Labor Party or an organization organized along such principles and advocating such tactics.

Up to the present time the members of the Left Wing in the Socialist Party have not formulated any definite policy of action; neither have they evolved concrete principles or tactics. Their whole activity has been one of sentimental sympathy and theoretical and tactical affinity to Bolshevism and the German Revolution. We believe, that the time has now arrived for the taking of a more definite stand. *Therefore, we now demand of these Socialists grouped around "The Revolutionary Age" and "The Class Struggle" to present their position on American affairs to the American working class.* We also again reiterate the question: Whether they will henceforth advocate secession of the revolutionary Socialists from the Socialist Party and affiliation with the Socialist Labor Party; if not, whether they will come out for the organization of a Communist Labor Party in America; or whether they will continue to practise this inconsistent policy of condemning Opportunism abroad and retaining membership in a party whose political record during the past year spreads a stench that would even drive a Scheidemann away. Furthermore, where do these Left-Wingers stand on the question of Socialist Industrial Unionism and the endorsation of the Workers' International Industrial Union—an organization firmly planted upon Socialist principles, recognizing the necessity of revolutionary industrial and political action? Will the large minority of Bolshevists and ultra-revolutionists "in European affairs" remain in the Socialist Party, a party which, through its Congressional Platform and disgusting conduct of elected representatives, is not even deserving of the name Opportunist; or will this minority, consistent with its cry for the revolutionary Dictatorship of the Proletariat, organize politically and industrially into organizations pledged and dedicated to the "unconditional surrender of the capitalist class" or "the lockout of the capitalist class from the industries"? This is the question of the hour! Comrades of the Left Wing, "The Revolutionary Age" and "The Class Struggle," we await your answer!

Revolutionary Socialism and the Constituent Assembly in Germany

> The seizure of state power by the proletariat, that means through a class of the people, cannot be artificially accomplished. It presupposes, aside from cases like the Paris Commune, where, exceptionally, the rulership fell into the proletariat's lap like property without a master, and not as the result of a conscious struggle, a fixed degree of ripeness in the politico-economic conditions. Here lies the main difference between Blanquistic coup d'états of a "resolute minority," which can be shot out of the mouth of a pistol, and, therefore, always arrives untimely, and the conquest of the state power through the large class-conscious mass of the people, which can itself only be a product of the beginning collapse of bourgeois society, and, consequently, carries within itself the politico-economic legitimacy of its timely appearance.
>
> *Rosa Luxemburg, in "Sozial-Reform oder Revolution," pages 13-14.*

ON JANUARY 19TH, the elections for the National Constituent Assembly take place in Germany. This is the date set by the National Soldiers' and Workingmen's Congress recently in session at Berlin. It is an election authorized by and conducted with the consent of the overwhelming majority of the German workers; it is also an election in which for the first time the women of Germany will participate on the basis of equal suffrage; and in consequence, this momentous electoral struggle bears all the earmarks and characteristics of full-fledged political Democracy. The elections to the Constituent Assembly symbolize one of the many significant fruits born by the Revolution; at least, so it appears to us. As Socialists or advocates of the highest expression of Democracy—Industrial Democracy, we consider political Democracy an indispensable asset in the waging of the class struggle; and Democracy, generally, in its broadest interpretation, an essential or imperative basic element of the proletarian movement. We hold with Wilhelm Liebknecht "that democracy is not a thing that is specifically political," and that "we must never forget that we are not merely a socialist party, but a social democratic party because we have perceived that socialism and democracy are inseparable."

Convinced that the ultimate victory of the proletariat is assured, because it is numerically by far the strongest class in society; also that the emancipation of the working class must be accomplished by the workers themselves; furthermore, knowing that our struggle for Industrial Democracy is in line with the visible trend and demand of social evolution, i. e., being conscious of the fact that the Socialist movement is ordained by historic development to be the steward of Democracy, we, therefore, greet the first manifestation of the class struggle conducted along the most advanced principles of political Democracy in this former citadel of feudal prerogatives with genuine pleasure, and consider the same a great stride forward in the direction of developing a genuine revolutionary Socialist movement in Germany.

However, not only are the elections to the National Constituent Assembly the first inaugurated by the Republic, i. e., the first called in the shadow of the great monarchical collapse, but, as a consequence, they are also the first to be contested by the workers in Germany as fully enfranchised citizens, as citizens whose social vision is no longer obscured by the many relatively irrelevant questions formerly prevalent at the elections, like such appertaining to constitutional reforms, etc., but whose political perspective is brought into direct contact with the issues and problems flowing from the economic and social divisions in present society—the class conflict. For the first time, the class conflict in Germany will be expressed clearly and sharply at the hustings; to quite a few workers the class struggle will now manifest itself as a distinct political struggle, a struggle no longer waged along the lines of compromise and palliation; because, for the first time in the history of Germany, a democratic election will take place, and workers organized as a distinct revolutionary party of Socialism will have the opportunity to contest the political supremacy of Capitalism, securely ambushed behind the Opportunism of the present government and the dictatorship of Allied Imperialism. The political struggle also furnishes splendid and exceptional opportunities to the revolutionary Socialists to expose the purely bourgeois Radicalism of the Opportunists, falsely flying the flag of Socialism, and to educate and organize the workers along revolutionary Socialist lines. The monumental question that now presents itself is: whether revolutionary Socialism is sufficiently emancipated from its former opportunistic affiliations, and sufficiently developed to comprehend the strategic value of its position in the elections; and also whether it is capable of appraising the inestimable value of an even minority representation

27

at this important historic Assembly to the future of the Socialist movement in Germany.

When studying the attitude of the three principal Socialist factions on the calling of the National Constituent Assembly, especially prior to the decision of the Soldiers' and Workingmen's Congress, we find that great disunity prevailed. We also detect the most vehement opposition to the elections and the Assembly amongst an element where we should least expect to find it—the Socialists constituting the recently organized Communist Labor Party. If the news is correct, the first convention of this party has, in the face of the decision of the S. and W. Congress, i. e., in the face of the majority vote of delegates representing the German proletariat, rejected Karl Liebknecht's motion to participate in the elections. We also glean from the reports that Rosa Luxemburg, who spoke against the Liebknecht resolution, is very emphatic in demanding another election to be held for delegates to the Local S. and W. Councils and the recently adjourned S. and W. Congress which she demands to remain in constant session.

Even the Independent Socialists at first opposed the convening of a National Constituent Assembly, because they considered the realization of Socialism via a Dictatorship of the Proletariat far less cumbersome and surer. Especially, when they were quite strongly represented in the Cabinet of the Ebert Government, this Dictatorship was considered quite a legitimate and feasible instrument for the inauguration of the Industrial Republic—as they conceived it.

Quite a few leaders of the Majority Socialists also looked with ill favor and apprehension upon not only a National Constituent Assembly, but also upon placing the fundamental power of government into the hands of the Soldiers' and Workingmen's Councils. However, when only skimming the surface of the political situation, we can appreciate that, primarily, the desire to concentrate and keep the power of government in the hands of a dictatorship did not grow so much out of the fear which certain Majority Socialists entertained for the voting strength of the reactionary and capitalist interests still strongly represented in the land, but rather out of the ominous terror that still takes possession of them, when they think of the general immaturity, especially in matters political, of the German workers. For instance, a man like Curt Eisner, Premier of the Bavarian Republic, declared himself AGAINST the immediate calling of the elections, because he considered the women at this stage incompetent to intelligently cast their ballots.

However, despite the undemocratic tendencies just observed, and in the face of these so absolutely unsocialistic dictatorial ambitions, the delegates to the S. and W. Congress were elected on the basis of a democratic suffrage, this assembly duly constituted itself as the representative convention or legislative and executive organ of the German working class, which it undoubtedly is, and adopted and proclaimed the call for the National Constituent Assembly against the insignificant vote of a minority seeking to establish the Dictatorship of revolutionary Socialism in place of the Dictatorship of Opportunism, however, strangely, not through the all-powerful channel of a class-conscious proletarian majority—but via the Blanquistic method of the coup d'état.

When studying the proceedings of the S. and W. Congress, we are also compelled to observe the sudden change in the attitude of the Independent Socialists from opponents to the Constituent Assembly to its supporters. The vote of the Independent Socialists for the motion setting January 19th as the date for the elections has been even condemned by certain elements in the Socialist movement as a betrayal of Socialist principles.

As has been amply set forth in our article on "The Revolution in Germany," the recent S. and W. Congress was a gathering completely controlled by the Opportunists in the labor movement. We also assume that we sufficiently explained the cause for this not at all extraordinary phenomenon. Nevertheless, considering the social composition of the gathering, and knowing that it was entirely composed of delegates elected by the German proletariat; knowing also that the elections to the S. and W. Congress were vigorously contested by the revolutionary Socialists; and knowing that the Opportunists, much to our regret, were practically victorious in all districts, therefore, reflecting, for the time at least, the will of the majority in the working class; we are compelled, again much to our regret, as firm adherents to the principles of Democracy, to recognize in the recent S. and W. Congress and the present Executive Council bodies officiating as the legitimate legislative and executive organs of the German working class; and must, therefore, as disciples of majority rule, again however much to our regret, also conceive in their decisions and decrees the bona fide Dictatorship of the Proletariat. However, as emphasized by us before, it is not the Revolutionary Socialist Dictatorship of the Proletariat which was in session or is governing now, not because the workers have been coerced into voting for the Opportunists, but because the German proletarian voters were not animated by revolutionary Socialist principles, i. e., were not revolutionary Socialists, and did not support the *Socialist* candidates. From the foregoing we can deduce that only revolutionary Socialists, forming the majority of the proletariat, can establish or launch the Revolutionary Dictatorship of the Proletariat.

Again emphasizing the essential democratic character of the Socialist movement, the unbending discipline and absolute obedience exacted by the dictatorship of the majority, we are, therefore, more than perturbed and rather doubtful as to the character of the Socialist principles and activities advocated and engaged in by certain opponents to the National Constituent Assembly. Especially, how in the shadow of the Peace Conference, with the German nation practically impotent from an industrial and military standpoint, a recognized Marxian scholar like Rosa Luxemburg and certain members of the Communist Labor Party can attempt to repudiate the call for the elections to the Constituent Assembly, and in the same breath expect support in a movement aiming to rebuild and re-elect the Local S. and W. Councils, two propositions absolutely at fisticuffs with each other, because one negates and the other affirms the rule of the soldiers and workingmen of Germany, and hope for success is more than we can comprehend. If the newspaper reports are correct, how a Rosa Luxemburg can consistently oppose a motion of Karl Liebknecht demanding that the Communist Labor Party contest the coming elections, and succeed in her opposition, thus denying to the minority of class-conscious Socialists the opportunity to express their interests and principles politically; thereby also greatly reducing the agitational and educational possibilities of this young organization; and, finally, how a student like Rosa Luxemburg can be instrumental in organizing a *political* party like the Communist Labor Party, a move which we certainly greeted with great joy, and then oppose an attempt of the young organization to enter the political arena as the vanguard of revolutionary Socialism is another manifestation we cannot understand. However, we sincerely trust that the reports, as has so often been the case, have been garbled, and that the Communist Labor Party, as the first political expression of revolutionary Socialism in Germany, is fearlessly and vigorously participating in the electoral struggle for the National Constituent Assembly; because to conclude with a quotation from Rosa Luxemburg, "The fate of democracy is, as we have seen, interwoven with the fate of the labor movement."

* * *

We are fully aware of the limitations set for the National Constituent Assembly. We are also aware that this gigantic electoral struggle, this inspiring plebiscite of *all* responsible men and women, will most likely end with a working majority for the Opportunists, i. e., will end by conferring additional power upon the Majority Socialists in the Constituent Assembly, and thus tend to cement or fasten the Dictatorship of Opportunism more firmly upon the German people. However, after a more than casual study of the present situation in Germany, the reader will also agree with us that any political government in Germany, even a government—assuming the possibility of the impossible— of the Spartacides, can only exercise certain *limited* functions,

30

functions more or less of an advisory and educational character; that, as an *independent* legislative and administrative body, the German Government, like all political organs, will be henceforth *dominated* not by the Dictatorship of Opportunism, but by the forces in *control* of the industrial resources or economic arteries of the country—Allied Imperialism.

Anglo-Saxon Imperialism practically exercises unlimited *economic sway* over Germany; the navy, fortresses, rolling stock, the opportunity for an effective blockade and even certain localities in which are located certain basic industries are in its hands. Anglo-Saxon Imperialism is, therefore, in possession of the forces upon which hinges the economic life of the German nation; consequently: to this industrial overlord the millions of voters in Germany must and do look for food and immediate relief.

This greedy and insatiable Imperialism is only awaiting the opportune moment to extend its despotic power; it is waiting for a "tangible reason," a "popular motive," which will furnish the opportunity to occupy additional German territory, and thus compellingly make German Imperialism, its former most dangerous competitor, subservient to its iron rule. This pretext or makeshift will be offered to the interests behind the armies now occupying certain German soil, if any but a responsible *democratic* government functions in Germany; if instead of the will of the majority, anarchy and the despotism of *unauthorized, irresponsible* minorities, no matter how altruistic their motives may be, reign. Therefore, the elections for the Constituent Assembly will serve as a powerful and constructive element to reduce and weaken the grip of Anglo-Saxon Imperialism upon the German people. All attempts to postpone or prevent the holding of these elections, which are synonymous with postponing or preventing the establishment of a representative government, i. e., all attempts to repudiate or break the sacred law formulated and adopted by the representatives of the German workers, by seeking to set up a dictatorship of pure and simple physical force, will not only prove disastrous to these modern Blanquists, but also offer the best possible basis to the Allied imperialists for a forceful and popular intervention—*"to safeguard law, order and the principles of DEMOCRACY," by reducing Germany to a vassal state.*

The Socialist Dictatorship of the Proletariat can only be reared by the proletariat, and only evolve out of and receive its mandate from a class-conscious majority of the working class. The Socialist Dictatorship of the Proletariat also announces the victory of Industrial Democracy at the hustings; it is a dictatorship that takes office and by so doing deposes itself; i. e., the Socialist Dictatorship of the Proletariat spells the abolition of the proletariat, the abolition of all economic classes, and the realization of the Industrial Republic. Such a dictatorship of *a class*

31

can only and must be inherently democratic, because its goal symbolizes the hightest potentiality of democratic endeavor—Industrial Democracy!

Therefore, hail to a democratized Germany; hail to the elections to the National Constituent Assembly; success to revolutionary Socialism at the hustings!